FAMILY LIFE IN
Ancient
Egypt

PETER CLAYTON

HODDER
Wayland

an imprint of Hodder Children's Books

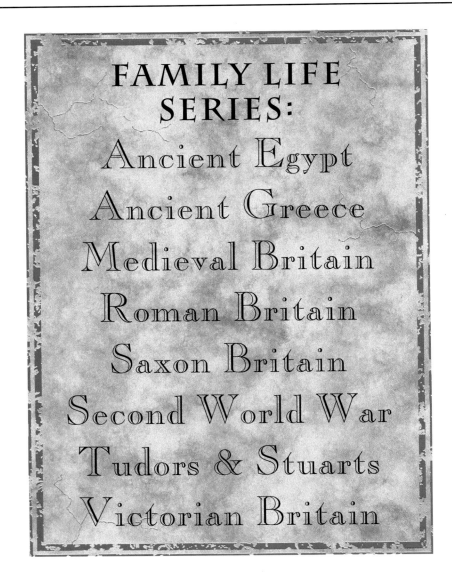

FAMILY LIFE
SERIES:

Ancient Egypt
Ancient Greece
Medieval Britain
Roman Britain
Saxon Britain
Second World War
Tudors & Stuarts
Victorian Britain

Series design: Pardoe Blacker Ltd
Editor: Katie Orchard
Production controller: Carol Stevens

**First published in 1995 by Wayland (Publishers) Ltd
This edition published in 2001 by Hodder Wayland,
an imprint of Hodder Children's Books**
© Hodder Wayland 1995

British Library Cataloguing in Publication Data
Clayton, Peter Arthur
 Family life in Ancient Egypt. – (Family Life series)
  I. Title II. Series
  306.850932

ISBN 0 7502 3519 5

Printed and bound by G. Canale & C. S.p.A. Turin, Italy

Cover pictures: The royal scribe, Ani, playing a board game; a jug and a small pottery statuette.

Picture acknowledgements: Peter Clayton *cover*, 5 (top and bottom), 6, 8 (top and bottom), 10 (left), 10-11 (bottom), 11 (right), 12, 14 (top and bottom), 15, 16 (top and bottom), 17, 18, 19 (top and bottom), 20, 21 (top and bottom), 22 (top), 24 (top and bottom), 25, 26 (left and right), 27, 28 (top and bottom), 29; C. M. Dixon 9 (Egyptian Museum, Cairo), 13 (bottom); Michael Holford 7, 22 (bottom), 23; Werner Forman Archive 13 top (Egyptian Museum, Cairo). Artwork on page 4 is by Nick Hawken.

CONTENTS

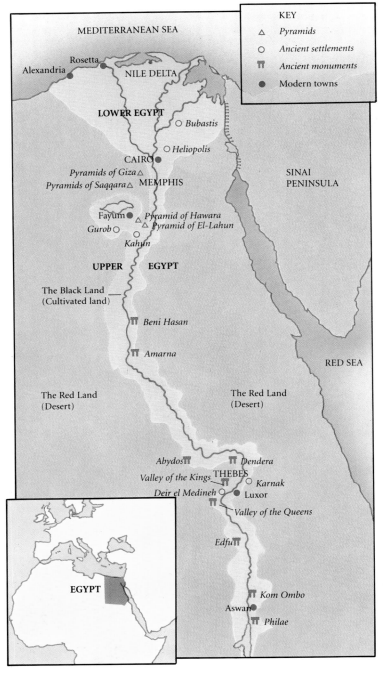

The Greek historian Herodotus, who visited Egypt in about 450 BC, wrote that Egypt had 'the gift of the Nile'. You only have to look at the map of Egypt to realize how true this is. As much as 94 per cent of Egypt is still desert. Only the narrow green strip of agricultural land alongside the river and the broader triangle in the **Delta**, where the river spreads out to enter the Mediterranean Sea, are fit to live in.

THE RED LAND AND THE BLACK LAND

The ancient Egyptians called their land Kemet – the Black Land – after the dark, fertile **silt** brought down by the Nile when it flooded each year during the **inundation**, from July to November. They called the **barren** desert, which they hated, Deshret – the Red Land.

Over 200,000 years ago, the earliest Egyptians lived by hunting the wild animals in the desert, and the water birds and animals that lived in the swampland beside the River Nile. It is believed that they moved about as tribes, made up of several family groups all living together and helping each other. There is very little archaeological evidence from this early period except for the **flint** tools which they used, such as hand axes, arrowheads and knives, that have been found on the high desert plain.

Only the narrow strip of fertile land beside the 1,546 km of the Nile in Egypt could support human life in ancient Egypt.

A view of the Nile in Middle Egypt at Beni Hasan, which clearly shows the strong division between the barren desert and the rich, green agricultural land.

The men hunted animals for food. The women cooked the family's food, made bread and used some of the animal skins to make clothing. After 3100 BC, some animal skins were still worn as religious dress – a priest would wear a leopard's skin and the **pharaoh** often had a bull's tail hanging from the back of his belt.

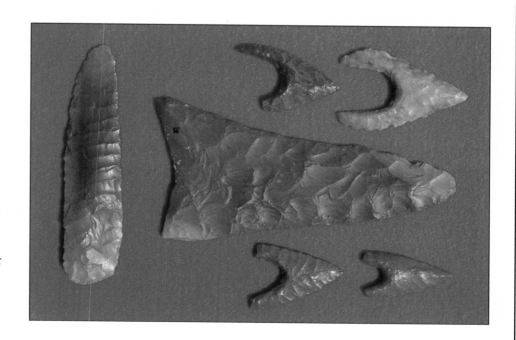

Flint tools made by prehistoric Egyptians before 4000 BC. They include hollow-backed arrowheads and two knives.

THE PEOPLE OF ANCIENT EGYPT

We do not know where the original ancient Egyptians came from. Some scholars argue that they came from Central Africa, others say that they came from the north of the Fertile Crescent, the area of northern Mesopotamia (modern-day Iraq) and Syria. **Civilization** grew up in the Nile Valley because families were able to survive there on the food that they could catch and with the help of a climate that was kind to them.

KINGS, NOBLES, PRIESTS AND SCRIBES

At the head of the people was the king (called the pharaoh after about 1450 BC), who was regarded as a living god on earth. Then there were the nobles and high-ranking families who served him. The structure of the people was rather like a pyramid, with the king at the top. Close to him were his nobles, and then below them, spreading out in order and in larger numbers, were the priests, followed by the scribes. To be able to read and write in ancient Egypt was very important for an educated person.

A wall painting from the tomb of the foreman Sennedjem at Deir el-Medineh from about 1250 BC, showing a priest wearing his ritual leopard skin, complete with the animal's head and claws.

(Right) The nobleman Nebamun, hunting in the marshes, on a fragment of a wall painting found in his tomb from about 1430 BC.

The backbone of Egyptian society consisted of the craftsmen and the peasants. Craftsmen taught their skills to their sons, who then followed their fathers' trades. Peasants, working in the **fertile** fields where they could get two, sometimes three, crops a year, supported the whole economy. They produced the food to feed everyone else and all the offerings that had to be made by the priests to the many different gods in the temples. The Egyptians believed that if they did not please the gods, the Nile would no longer rise each year. This would mean that the crops and animals would die, and the pharaohs would no longer be able to speak to the gods on the people's behalf.

FAMILIES

Peasant families working in the fields were an important group of people, because unless they all worked together they could not survive. Higher-class families of professional people and nobles and, of course, the royal family, were tied together more by their blood relationship than by a need for them to work together. The whole of ancient Egyptian society was based on the structure of the family. Even the many gods and goddesses were all related in small family groups, usually of father, mother and son.

(Above) A statuette from around 2475 BC of the dwarf, Seneb, with his wife Senetites and their young son and daughter. Seneb was chief of all the palace dwarfs in charge of the royal wardrobe.

The Overseer of Workmen, Ankherkhau, dressed in fine linen clothes and seated with his wife and his four young daughters. This wall painting in his tomb was painted in about 1160 BC.

MEN

In Egyptian families, men were thought to have more importance than women. Sons were also very important because they would carry on farming the family's land, or learn their father's profession, being taught by him as an apprentice. If a man was Chief Sculptor, then his son became Chief Sculptor after him.

'If a man's son accepts his father's words,
No plan of his will go wrong.
Teach your son to be a hearer.'

A coloured relief, from about 1900 BC, of the nobleman Imn-n-hat and his wife. They are seated on a bench with their son Intef between them and, nearby, an offering table piled high with food that includes a leg of meat, bread and onions.

Old age was respected and so a grandfather, or even a great-grandfather, remained as the head of the household until he died. Peasants did not expect to live very long by our standards, probably not later than into their thirties. Wealthier people lived longer – two pharaohs lived into their nineties, but that was very unusual.

9

WOMEN

Girls married early, usually from about the age of eleven, and generally to older men who could support them. Although the life of a woman was hard, she was normally well cared for and also independent. Anything that she brought to the marriage, such as property or possessions, remained hers. If the husband died, the widow was entitled to a third of her husband's property and part of what they may have held jointly. Divorce was not complicated and could happen for many different reasons. The couple would separate and the wife would return to her parents' home. She could then marry again if she wanted to.

A finely made red pottery vase in the shape of a mother nursing a small child, from about 1400 BC.

A wooden model showing women in a weaving shed, working a loom on the floor. The standing women are spinning wool. This model was buried in the tomb of Chancellor Meket-Re in about 2050 BC.

Egypt was a 'matrilineal' society, which means that the family line went through the mother. The mother was therefore very important – people would normally know who their mother was, but possibly not their father. Amongst the royal family, the senior queen and her daughters, the princesses, carried the continuity of the royal blood line. That is why royal marriages between brothers and sisters and other close relatives are known at times during this period. This did not normally happen in ordinary families.

A woman who was unfaithful to her husband was harshly punished, because she was upsetting the family system. She could even be put to death and her body would be burned. As if this were not bad enough, it also meant that she could not then expect an afterlife amongst the gods.

A red pottery vase, in the shape of a woman playing a small lute, from about 1360 BC. It was probably used for cosmetics.

MARRIAGE

There was no religious or legal ceremony for two people to marry – in fact, there is no word in ancient Egyptian that means 'wedding'. Marriages were arranged by the parents of the bride and groom agreeing to the match. The girl would then leave her father's house to go to her new home. She was accompanied by a large procession (it still happens today in the villages of Egypt), and this showed everyone that the couple were 'married'.

'When you prosper and found your house,
And love your wife with ardour,
Fill her belly, clothe her back,
Ointment soothes her body.
Gladden her heart as long as you live.'

Painted limestone seated statues from about 2620 BC, of the prince Rahotep and his wife, the princess Nofret. Notice her fine bead collar and jewelled headband.

Marriages with foreigners were not frowned upon, and there are representations of Egyptian women with foreign **mercenary** soldiers as husbands. A close relation or even a slave could be taken as a partner. Only death or divorce could separate a couple, but there is not much written evidence of divorces in Egypt until Graeco-Roman times (from about 300 BC – AD 300).

CHILDREN

Children were very important to the ancient Egyptian family. A woman who produced many children was respected in the community, and children were expected to look after their parents in their old age – it was their duty. If a couple could not have any children, then they could adopt them. Because many women died in childbirth (as it was quite dangerous), there were often orphans who would be glad to be accepted into a family that wanted them.

(Above) A relief showing the inlaid back panel of Tutankhamun's throne, from about 1330 BC. It shows the young pharaoh with his wife, Ankhesenamun, who is smoothing perfumed oil on her husband's broad collar from a small cup in her left hand.

(Right) The pharaoh Akhenaten and his wife Nefertiti, under the protection of the rays of Aten (the sun god), play with three of their small daughters. This relief is from about 1345 BC.

Children are often represented in tomb wall paintings, but usually they are shown as small versions of young adults. One sign of youth was the way a child's hair was cut: both girls and boys had a 'sidelock of youth'. This was a tress of hair left hanging on one side of their heads. Noble and royal children had this carefully dressed and often wore a precious metal ornament or clasp on it.

This wall painting, from about 1290 BC, from the tomb of the prince Amenhirkhopshef, shows the sidelock of youth which all children wore. The prince is dressed in fine linen clothes and has a jewelled clasp to hold his sidelock in place. He is standing behind his father, Ramesses III.

CLOTHES

The hot, dry climate in Egypt meant that not many clothes were needed. Men wore a short kilt and had a warm cloak for evening or the cooler months. Women's dresses were usually made of a single piece of linen, and children often went naked. Better-off families, like those of nobles, priests and scribes, had many more clothes, but these were also usually made of linen (wool was rarely used in ancient Egypt).

There were many different kinds of linen used, from coarse weave to fine, almost transparent cloth. Bright, natural colours were used to dye the clothes of the rich. Many fashions, especially in the eighteenth and nineteenth dynasties (around 1400 – 1000 BC), were very elegant, with wraps and draped shawls. The clothes were kept in special boxes and these have sometimes been found in tombs, as in that of the **architect** Kha at Deir el-Medineh. In the tomb of the boy king Tutankhamun, a whole series of changes of clothes, kilts and bed linen were preserved.

An elegantly shaped, small clothes chest from about 1250 BC, which, according to the inscription on the lid, belonged to an Egyptian sea captain named Daneg-Ro.

LESSONS

Educated people who could read and write hieroglyphs were known as scribes. They were more highly respected than people who could only do manual work. Scribes are represented in tomb paintings, carvings and statues. They are always working and alert. A father, Dua-Khety told his son, Pepy, that every other job had something wrong with it: a soldier could get killed, a 'weaver inside the weaving house is more wretched than a woman', a potter 'is covered with earth', and so on. However, it was believed that if a child could read and write, he or she would have a more successful life. This is how Dua-Khety instructed Pepy as he took him to the 'school of writings among the children of the magistrates':

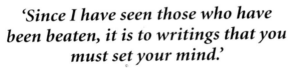

'Since I have seen those who have been beaten, it is to writings that you must set your mind.'

This small wooden statuette, from about 1900 BC, shows a scribe busy at his writing board.

*A detail from the **Book of the Dead** of the royal scribe Ani, showing him playing a board game called senet, which was rather like draughts. This is painted on **papyrus**, and dates from about 1250 BC.*

16

The only lessons given to the children of people who worked in the fields – which meant most of the population – would come from their fathers, who would teach them how to be a farmer, how to look after their animals and how to be part of their community.

A wall painting from the tomb of the nobleman Nebamun, from about 1430 BC. This shows women at a banquet clapping their hands in time to the double-flute player. The cones on their heads contain perfumed myrrh, which melted to give off a scent.

GAMES AND PARTIES

Not all life was harsh. Children played games, but mostly amongst themselves rather than with toys. There were rag dolls and simple balls, hoops and sticks, but little else for amusement. Wealthier people enjoyed parties and banquets. Many of these scenes were painted in the tombs, in the hope that life would be just like that in the next world. Children often went to the parties with their parents and are shown standing beside their father's or mother's chair, often holding a pet animal or bird in their hands.

AT HOME

The Egyptian family house was very simple, built of sun-dried mud-bricks. In an agricultural village, the houses were clustered together with narrow lanes winding in between them. Villages like Deir el-Medineh, Thebes, had a narrow main street which all the houses opened on to, and an even narrower alleyway behind the houses.

The royal scribe Nakht, and his wife Tjiui, stand in front of their typically Egyptian house, with its few windows set high in the walls to keep the interior cool. This is a detail from their painted papyrus Book of the Dead, from around 1320 BC.

Each house had a large main room that opened directly on to the street and a smaller room behind that. Some of the houses had cellars. Others had stairs going up to the roof, because people would sleep there during very hot weather.

Nobles' houses had wooden columns to support the roof, and usually there was a large garden around the house, with a pool in it. The royal palaces were also built of mud-brick, and stone was used only for column bases and door thresholds.

FOOD AND COOKING

Food was very simple, mainly vegetables of many different kinds, especially onions because the crops were so plentiful. Unleavened bread, (made from round, flattened wads of dough), was the other basic part of the diet.

The average family rarely ate meat, except small animals they might catch in the fields or desert, or birds caught at the river bank. Professional people ate better, especially the priests, because meat offerings were made to the gods in the temples and the priests could eat the meat afterwards. There are many scenes on tomb walls of butchers at work carving joints and legs off large bulls for the temples, of geese and ducks being fed, of trappers with nets catching birds in the fields, and of men fishing on the Nile from papyrus **skiffs**.

Cooking was done in simple, clay-built ovens, often in the open air, but as a lot of the foods were vegetables, they were usually eaten raw.

A stone statuette from about 2325 BC, showing a woman grinding corn by rubbing it on a sloping stone board.

A small wooden model of a pair of papyrus skiffs, dragging a trawl net between them with their catch of fish in it. This model came from the tomb of Chancellor Meket-Re, from about 2050 BC.

19

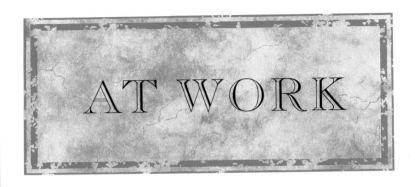

AT WORK

CRAFTSMEN AND BUILDERS

In the social **hierarchy** below the nobles, priests and scribes came the craftsmen and builders, men who had been taught their trades for generations by their fathers. They would include people such as artists, sculptors and carpenters. We can see all of them at work in the tomb paintings, and many examples of their actual work have survived and can be seen in museums. Builders using mud-bricks and shaping stone blocks are also shown in the paintings. These skilled men may have worked away from their villages and families for long periods at a time, wherever work was to be found.

The carpenters in this model, from the tomb of Chancellor Meket-Re from about 2050 BC, are busy sawing and shaping wood.

The names of ancient Egyptian artists, sculptors, architects or builders are not generally known because they were regarded simply as craftsmen doing their jobs. There are occasional exceptions, like Imhotep, **vizier** and chief architect to King Zoser. He built the first stone building in the world for his master, the Step Pyramid at Saqqara, in about 2670 BC. In later times, Imhotep was respected as a god of architecture and also of medicine.

This model shows how early Egyptian small glass vessels were made by heating special sand in an open furnace, made hotter by the men using long blowpipes.

*This wall painting, from about 1250 BC, comes from the tomb of Sennedjem, who worked on the royal tombs. It shows him ploughing in the **Afterworld** with a pair of yoked oxen while his wife Iyneferti follows behind, scattering the corn seed.*

FARMERS

Agricultural work in the fields was hard and the hours were long; the peasants, including most of their families, would work from sunrise to sunset with a break at the hottest part of the day. The peasants were supervised constantly by overseers and scribes, as the tomb paintings show us.

Because of the climate in ancient Egypt there were only three seasons: inundation, sowing, and harvest. The cycle would then start all over again. When the peasants could not work on the land because of the flood, they were often employed on other projects, such as building the pyramids during the period 2700 – 2100 BC.

Sennedjem harvests the fine crop of corn in the Afterworld and his wife gathers up the dropped husks of corn behind him in this painting from about 1250 BC.

Cattle were driven around on the harvested corn to thresh it and separate the wheat ears from the stalks, as this copy of a wall painting from the tomb of Menna shows us.

When the annual floods had settled down, the first thing to be done was to replace the **property boundary markers**. Then the land had to be ploughed and new seed planted. The husband would do the ploughing, and his wife would follow, scattering the seed behind him. Sometimes an older child would do this. When the harvest began to sprout, surveyors and scribes – the tax inspectors – would come to look at the size of the crop and see how much of it would have to be given up as tax.

This modern copy of a painting in the tomb of Menna shows men using shallow wooden scoops to toss the corn ears into the air (winnowing), to separate the last of the chaff.

When harvest time came, everyone was very busy. The corn had to be cut, and again the wife would follow her husband as he reaped, bending over to pick up the fallen and missed husks of wheat.

Then the wheat had to be **threshed**, the corn ears broken down, and then **winnowed**, usually by tossing them into the air using special wooden shovels, for the breeze to separate and remove the husks. Next, the harvest was taken to the granaries, to be ground into flour for bread. Everyone in the family was involved in various ways in all these tasks.

TOWNS AND VILLAGES

Very few ancient Egyptian town sites have been **excavated**, because most of the excavations carried out have been concerned with tombs and temples. Therefore, not very much is known about the different towns that must have existed. One special town that is known was Kahun, which was built by King Senusret II (1897 – 1878 BC) for the craftsmen and workmen building his pyramid nearby. Here, in AD 1887, the **Egyptologist** Flinders Petrie found many objects of everyday use still in the houses where they had been left when the workforce moved on.

Only tombs and temples were permanent structures in ancient Egypt. Even in the royal palaces (seen here at Medinet Habu), only the thresholds of doorways and column bases were made of stone. Everything else was made of mud-brick.

(Left) These small houses built close together form the workers' village at Deir el-Medineh, it is one of the few sites of ordinary houses that have been excavated in Egypt.

Another workers' village was at Deir el-Medineh. The workmen who lived there were employed to dig and to decorate the royal tombs in the Valley of the Kings. Archaeologists have been able to learn a great deal from Deir el-Medineh, where many details of family life were found – letters, sketches, literary texts and details of local scandals and complaints about neighbours.

The mud-brick lower walls surviving in the great northern royal palace at el-Amarna, capital of the pharaoh Akhenaten (1350 – 1334 BC), are over 3,000 years old. They were originally covered with beautifully painted coloured plaster. Only the circular bases for the wooden columns were made of stone.

Because so few towns have been excavated, we do not have plans of them showing market-places, as in the Greek and Roman worlds, but there were markets. Since money was not used in ancient Egypt (it had not been invented), all deals were done by bartering, or exchanging goods.

Great cities such as the capital, Memphis, and the religious centres such as Thebes and other towns grew up around the major temples. Generally, however, little is known about these because most buildings, other than stone-built temples, were not built to last – not even the royal palaces.

GODS AND TEMPLES

The worship of the gods influenced everyone's lives – their homes, families and food. The family structure was reflected amongst the gods, the chief of whom was Amun, with his wife Mut and their son Khonsu. There were other families amongst the gods. For the ordinary Egyptian, the most important of these families was the God of the Dead Osiris, his wife Isis and their son Horus.

In the home, one particular god, Bes, was worshipped as the guardian of women and children, and he was also the god of music and merriment. He was usually represented as misshapen and small, with short, stubby legs, a funny, almost ferocious face with lion's whiskers, and a tall, plumed head-dress.

Isis was the most important Egyptian goddess and this bronze statuette, from 664 – 525 BC, shows her nursing her young son Horus.

The strange-looking god Bes was believed to protect women and children, as well as being a god of merriment and music. This stone carving is from about 305 – 30 BC.

Temples were called 'the fortresses of the gods' because they were huge and built from stone. Ordinary people never went inside them – only the priests and the king were allowed into these holy places. Whilst the temple might be dedicated to a particular god, the people would only be aware of that god on official holidays, when everyone had time off to attend the great religious processions.

Every Egyptian temple had a sacred lake where the priests could wash and where they would sail the god's ship. This one is in the temple of the chief god Amun-Re at Karnak.

One such holiday was the Festival of Opet, when the statue of the god Amun-Re was taken from the innermost sanctuary of his temple on a sacred boat, and carried on the shoulders of the priests in a procession. The procession went from his great temple at Karnak to his other nearby temple, five kilometres away, at Luxor. People lined the streets, musicians played and everyone enjoyed the festival. It was the only time that ordinary people could be involved directly in their religion. They could then make requests to the god's statue as it passed by, and he might answer by making his sacred boat tip or turn to acknowledge or refuse the request.

THE NEXT WORLD

The ancient Egyptians believed that when they died, they went on a long journey to the next world and had to be prepared for it in their burial with food and drink. The very early graves were simply a hole scooped in the sand, where the body would be surrounded by food and drink offerings from the family to help the soul on its journey. Some ornaments, jewellery or weapons might also be added. If the dead person's family was wealthy enough, the body was **mummified** and placed in a rock-cut tomb with all his or her possessions.

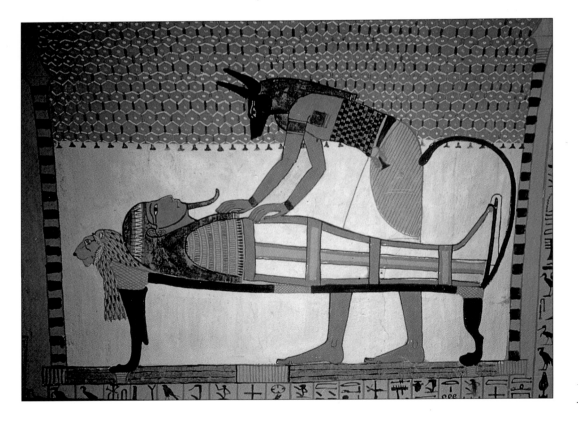

In the tomb of Sennedjem, Anubis, the jackal-headed god of embalming prepares his mummy for the next world.

(Left) From the very earliest times the Egyptians believed that the dead had to take things with them on the long journey to the Afterworld. This ancient Egyptian died over 6,000 years ago and was buried with pots of drink, meat, and his necklaces.

Very few tombs have been found completely intact; most had been robbed many years before being rediscovered by archaeologists. Many were family tombs, reopened only to place another member of the family there.

The ancient Egyptians believed that all the family could be united in the next world. When someone died, before he or she could enter the Egyptian equivalent of heaven, 'the Fields of Iarru', he or she had to pass an examination – the 'Weighing of the Heart' – to see if the person was suitable. The heart would be weighed in a balance against the Feather of Truth, which represented the Goddess of Truth, Ma'at. This was done to see if he or she had been a good person on earth.

This scene is often represented in the papyrus Books of the Dead. The dead person had to give a truthful answer to forty-two questions, each one asked by a different god. If successful, he or she was then presented before the God of the Dead, Osiris, as being 'Ma'at heru' – 'True of Voice' and was worthy of entering the blessed next world. Joyous reunions could then be made with dead family members.

It is from these carved and painted scenes that we know so much about ancient Egypt and daily family life there, three and four thousand years ago.

This detail from the papyrus Book of the Dead of the royal scribe Ani, from about 1250 BC, shows his heart being weighed against the Feather of Truth.

GLOSSARY

Afterworld Egyptians believed they would go on to another world after they died.

Architect Someone who designs buildings.

Barren Unable to support any life.

Book of the Dead A papyrus scroll (not really a book) on which was written a collection of prayers or spells that would help and protect the dead person in the next world.

Civilization The fully developed culture of a society.

Delta The flat, silty area of some rivers where the main river splits up to form lesser rivers.

Egyptologist Someone who studies the history of ancient Egypt.

Excavated To be dug up from the ground.

Fertile Having soil rich enough to support a thriving plant population.

Flint A hard, sharp stone used to make tools.

Hierarchy A strict order of importance.

Inundation The annual flooding of the Nile (until 1900, when a dam was built at Aswan), when the water began to rise in July and spread silt over the land, subsiding in November, when the seed could be planted.

Mercenary A soldier who was willing to fight for any side that paid him. In ancient Egypt mercenaries were usually foreign troops.

Mummified When the dead body was preserved for burial to appear lifelike.

Papyrus A tall, riverside reed that grew wild in Egypt. It was cut and the stalk slit into thin strips which were beaten together, criss-cross, to make sheets about 30 cm^2. Several squares could be joined together and made into a long roll.

Pharaoh A word we use to describe an ancient Egyptian king. It is made up of two ancient Egyptian words, 'per aoh', which mean 'The Great House'.

Property boundary markers Markers which are used to surround someone's property, to show that he or she owns it.

Silt A rich mud, made up of debris from the bottom of a river.

Skiff A small boat, rather like a canoe.

Threshing Beating ripe stalks of corn or wheat so that the grain is separated from the husks and straw.

Vizier A man who was second only to the pharaoh, and who could act on his behalf when he was away. He was often a close relative of the pharaoh.

Winnowing Using wind or air currents to separate the grain from the husks and straw of corn or wheat.

BOOKS TO READ

Coote, Roger, *The Egyptians* (Wayland, 1993)
Janssen, Jac J. and Rosalind M. *Growing up in Ancient Egypt* (Rubicon Press, 1990)
Oliphant, Margaret, *The Egyptian World* (Kingfisher Books, 1989)
Quirke, Stephen and Spencer, Jeffrey, *The British Museum Book of Ancient Egypt* (British Museum Press, 1992)
Vercoutter, Jean, *The Search for Ancient Egypt* (Thames and Hudson, 1992)

PLACES TO VISIT

Ashmolean Museum, Beaumont Street, Oxford OX1 2PH.
A very good collection that exhibits many aspects of daily life in its Egyptian galleries.

British Museum, Great Russell Street, London WC1B 3DG.
The largest and finest collection of all kinds of Egyptian antiquities in Britain.

Fitzwilliam Museum, Trumpington Street, Cambridge CB2 1RB.
Many ancient Egyptian works of art.

Manchester Museum, Oxford Road, Manchester M13 9PL.
Several newly displayed Egyptian galleries.

Petrie Museum, University College London, Malet Place, London WC1.
A collection of objects of everyday Egyptian life.

ABROAD

On holidays, there are splendid ancient Egyptian collections to be seen:
Egypt:
Cairo Egyptian Museum.
France:
Paris (Louvre Museum).
Germany:
Berlin (Ägyptisches Museum).
Munich (Staatlichen Sammlung Ägyptischer Kunst Museum).
Holland:
Leiden (National Museum).
Italy:
Florence (Archaeological Museum).
Rome (Vatican Museums).
Turin (Archaeological Museum).

INDEX

Figures in **bold** are illustrations. Glossary entries are shown by the letter g.